The

Incredible Power

of

Simple
Service

Hi Birute
and Gerry!
Thanks so much
for your interest in
the book, I hope that
you enjoy! It is my prayer that
God might use this little book
for His glory.

Love you guys,

Bill

(Luke 16:13)

. . . a story of losing and finding purpose in life . . .

The

Incredible Power

of

Simple
Service

Bill Mulligan

Contents

With Thanks

While the writing of *The Incredible Power of Simple Service* was primarily a solitary experience, the editing, formatting, graphics creation, and promotion of the book is quite a team effort. Without the help of many others, the book you are holding would have never progressed to a finished product.

At the risk of forgetting someone who helped and is not mentioned, here are a few folks that I want to recognize. To these people I am forever grateful.

Given her close proximity to me, living in the same house during a pandemic, my wife, Rosemary, was the first person to read many of my early thoughts as I contemplated the writing of a book. I would typically write early in the day and then, each evening, ask Rosemary to review what I had written. My earliest thoughts were often rough around the edges, but Rosemary endured and encouraged me from beginning to end.

Right behind Rosemary, Jim Holmes and his team at Great Writing joined the effort. Simply stated, without Jim's help and direction in editing, formatting, and graphic creation, this book would not exist. It took every ounce of creative energy in my body to deliver a transcript to Jim, who then took my very rough effort and transformed it into a book.

Somewhere early in the process, a few very close family members and friends pitched in by reading my early writing. Again, these early versions had some spelling and grammatical errors, but my faithful friends pressed on and provided some great feedback. Included in that group of early supporters is my sister, Susan, who has read the text multiple times in an effort to find every last typo or error. A huge thank you to Susan for her eye for detail, and especially for her encouragement from the beginning to the end of the project.

A special shout out to my son, Billy, who rounds out this family-and-friends effort for his help with promotion and all things related to social media. If you are not a friend or family member, and you are enjoying this book, it is because of Billy's help in getting the word out.

Most important, I thank the God who created me for giving me the time, energy, presence of mind, and resources needed to commit my thoughts to print.

Cleveland Fall Technical Conference

"We like to wind up our sales associates and watch them go."

Let every soul be subject to the governing authorities, for
there is no authority except from God, and the authorities
that exist are appointed by God.

Romans 13:1

• • • • • • • • • • •

My boss called me in mid-September to let me know that he was assigning me to attend the 2018 fall technical conference at the end of October. The meeting site was Cleveland.

Yes, Cleveland at the end of October. The Indians would not be playing baseball, the Cavaliers had long since said goodbye to LeBron and the Browns. . . well you know about the Browns. We could have gone to the Rock and Roll Hall of Fame but we feared for our jobs that word would get back to the home office that we had actually taken an evening off and had some fun.

I liked my boss; he was a great guy. In his words, he wanted to "share the love." As some of my co-workers had just attended other conferences, he wanted to be sure that I didn't feel slighted. The truth is that the conferences that I *didn't attend* were the better opportunities—by a long shot. One was in Chicago, a longstanding *must-attend* event for anyone in our industry; I hadn't missed one in recent memory. The other was more of a vacation, held at a high-end luxury property at Amelia Island. Most attendees took their spouses. I went to Cleveland with my technical guy. Our Cleveland hotel was the kind of place where you might contract Legionnaires' disease—and that's not exactly "sharing the love."

Just for good measure, I made the six-hour drive on a Sunday afternoon as the conference started bright and early on Monday morning.

Speaking of bright and early Monday morning, I get a call from a great friend from our industry. Let's call him Walter.

Walter asks me if I am in Cleveland, and my spirits are immediately lifted as Walter tells me that *he* is in Cleveland. Walter works hard, plays hard, and he knows everyone. In my mind, I am thinking, "Here is my lifeline; I can catch up with Walter and salvage something good out of this potentially dead-end conference—well, not quite dead-end."

Walter explains that he is in Cleveland but that his company hasn't wasted the money to register him for the conference as he had the advance intelligence indicating that fewer than ten prospects had registered for the program. In summary, this was going to be a "supplier fest" and a total waste of time and money. So much for catching up with Walter. . .

As the three-day conference played out, Walter was correct. There were very few prospects and there was lots of technical information that I, as a salesperson, had very little interest in. My purpose here was to focus on the tabletop exhibits where we had hoped to actually "sell" something.

Regarding "selling," just by way of background I should mention that the product that I was selling was an engraved roller that is a critical component in all package printing products. Just so you know, any printed packaging that you have in your home—whether labels, fast-food bags, cereal boxes, or personal care products, etc.—utilizes this engraved roller to deliver ink to the print plate.

Perspective:

I am to obey my superiors. Romans 13:1 tells me to *obey the "authorities";* in my mind, that includes those whom I report to in the workplace. Verse 2 of the same passage says, *"Therefore whoever resists the authority resists the ordinance of God, and those who resist will bring judgment on themselves."* That's pretty straightforward and somewhat concerning to me as a guy who never met a boss I didn't like to tangle with.

For those who know me best, or even know me just a little, I struggle with authority—specifically in the workplace. In the workplace, the only position worse than mine is that of the guy whom I report to. One of my character defects is this lack of appreciation for the poor guy, the guy who has to give me my marching orders. I can't explain it, but I can confess the sin and commit to improving myself.

I will say that, over the years, I have matured and gotten better to some degree in this area. In this case, I was particularly blessed to be reporting to a man who knew me well, recognized my struggle in this area, and made it easier for me to take the Cleveland assignment with a better attitude than I might have had earlier in life.

I attribute whatever growth I have attained in this area primarily to God's grace. Ephesians 2:8–9 says, *"For by grace you have been saved through faith, and that not of yourselves; it is the gift of God, not of works, lest anyone should boast."* So, just to be crystal clear before we proceed with this story, by the grace of God and through the shed blood of His Son Jesus Christ, I was saved in 1993. It had nothing to do with me; it was a gift, there was nothing I could do to "earn it," and I count this to be the most important event of my life. Nothing else comes close. I need to emphasize that any growth that I demonstrate is clearly a result of God's grace, and conversely any sin in my life is evidence of the traitor still living within me.

Application:

The world tells us this:
"When life gives you lemons, make lemonade."
God's Word tells you that when your boss gives you a loser
assignment, you should remember that He put that boss in
a position to direct you, and the best response you can make
is to follow that direction.

⚘

The Big One: "You Are from Where?"

"Remember, I'm behind you all the way.
WAY behind you."

His lord said to him, "Well done, good and faithful servant;
you have been faithful over a few things, I will make you
ruler over many things. Enter into the joy of your lord."

Matthew 25:23

• • • • • • • • • • •

It's Wednesday, the last day of the least productive days of recent memory in Cleveland. I struggle to stay focused through
the morning's technical presentations, plow through the
standard issue lunch buffet, and proceed to the exhibition
hall to man our tabletop for one last day of what feels like
watching paint dry.

It bears mentioning here that I have been in my particular
industry for forty-two years. Yes, I am that old! While I could
not possibly know everyone in my industry, I consider myself
as well-connected as anyone. So at an event like this, by the
third day, I have sized up the crowd and split the delegates
into a few categories:

- People I know who are current customers;
- People I know who are not customers and probably
  never will be;
- People that I don't know.

In this "crowd" of ten prospects, by my count there are
four customers, four that will never be customers, and two
that I don't know.

So here we are at the end of the third day and two guys
whom I do not recognize approach our booth. To add to the
moderate intrigue, I don't recognize the company name on
their name badges. Incidentally, as a seasoned salesperson,
I have perfected the unique ability in about ten seconds to
read a name badge, observe the person's dress code and
body language, and make a snap decision about his value.

I am not proud of this judgmental exercise; it's one of those aspects of the job that I perform.

This snap profiling is a breeze with these two guys. Dressed in khakis, plaid button-down shirts, and the dead giveaway steel tip hikers, these two are evidently engineers. They do a good job of profiling me as well; they instantly see me as the sales guy, avoid me like the plague, and engage with my tech guy.

I stand far enough away so as to not get sucked into a technical discussion, but close enough to hear anything that might be of interest to me. As I listen, it seems to me that these two guys might not even be at the right conference. They are not in the package printing business; they are from the renewable-energy industry. By now, I am equal parts amused and frustrated that the best prospect that has come our way in three days most certainly will never need the product that we sell!

But hold the phone—there's a glimmer of hope. I overhear that these guys actually do use an engraved roller *similar* to what we manufacture; not exactly, but similar. Due to a signed non-disclosure agreement, I can't give many details, but in a million years I would never have guessed that these guys would have an application that we could discuss.

Now in true sales-guy mode, I have to wiggle my way into the conversation without appearing to be too self-serving. At the same time as I am trying to edge my way in, a sidebar situation is developing. We had another sales guy at the conference and he has started to smell a potential sale, so I have to edge him out as well. (Did I mention that the sales profession is a dirty job?) I quickly dispense of the other sales guy—easy enough to do on a technicality related to the prospect's application. I assure my colleague that this prospect is mine—and he should get lost!

In a very short ensuing conversation, I realize the tremendous error of my snap-profiling exercise. Not only are these guys viable prospects, but the potential of their account is huge—bigger than anything I had entertained in my entire career!

Their application was not only potentially huge; it was unique and very different from everything that we do for our other clients. All of a sudden, that six-hour drive back to my home office became much more interesting. During those six hours in the car, the wheels in my head were working overtime, formulating a plan of attack. The clock was ticking, as I knew that these two engineers had talked to all five of my competitors who were at the conference.

PERSPECTIVE:

Be faithful in the little things.

The parable of the talents from Matthew 25 says: *His lord said to him, "Well done, good and faithful servant; you have been faithful over a few things, I will make you ruler over many things. Enter into the joy of your lord."*

I am the master of the little things. If nothing else I am obsessive-compulsive, and I attend to the details better than most anyone. . . to the point of exhaustion! This has served me well in my career but not so well in my personal relationships; the people who know me best consider my OCD to be an annoyance.

In this case, I felt that my ship had come in. For years, I had "done the right" thing with all of the little things. I treated the smallest customer the same way that I treated the largest. Many of my counterparts did not subscribe to the same thinking; the small customers were a necessary evil and were treated accordingly. Many in the sales profession are primarily interested in the "big fish," the "home run," or the "granddaddy of all accounts." Pick your metaphor; most salespeople are looking for the larger accounts.

So for me, I felt this a vindication of sorts, as I had "played the right way" and now the reward was being laid out right in front of me. To quote the parable: *"You have been faithful over a few things, I will make you ruler over many things."* I had been faithful over the few things and I was now about to be the ruler over many. You could not make this stuff up. After many years of hard work and determination, I was positioned to be at the top of the heap! For good measure, all of this was happening as I neared the end of my working career.

APPLICATION:

....

Large or small, great or little, we need to be extremely careful with what God sends our way.

☙

Be Careful What You Ask For

"You forgot the 'rags' in your 'rags to riches' story."

*For what profit is it to a man if he gains the whole world,
and loses his own soul? Or what will a man give in exchange for his soul?*

Matthew 16:26

• • • • • • • • • • •

Of all the parts of the sales process, my favorite part is the hunt. The "hunt" involves prospecting, qualifying, and developing a plan of action that leads to the close of the sale. So in this case, we found our prospect in Cleveland, qualified him in short order, and as this opportunity was now for real, we needed to formulate a plan of action.

I have always realized that sales was a team game and not a solo effort. In summary, I was only as good as the team that I was a part of. Over the years, I have been part of good teams, bad teams, and teams that were somewhere in between. At this point in time, my team was somewhere in between. The company that I represented had a great legacy in our industry, but the third-generation ownership leading the company at the time was suspect, to say the least.

Coming out of the factory, the finished product was above average, but getting to the finished product was most times a challenge. We were short staffed internally, overworked, and morale was not good. Fortunately, we could still tell a good story and the facility and team still showed well when we brought prospects into our building to demonstrate our capabilities. We also showed favorably when compared to our competition. Lastly, because our prospect was not from our industry, news of the dirty laundry that was starting to leak out about our declining company was limited to our industry segment (print and packaging) and not the segment (renewable energy) that my prospect was from.

The formulation of the plan was a two-man effort, comprising of me and the man that I reported to. In hindsight, this was our first mistake, but, in defense, we had no choice. We found little or no support from the rest of the team as most didn't believe that the project would ever materialize. In defense of the other team members, for years they had all heard from salespeople like me that this was "the big one, blah, blah, blah." A secondary concern, internally, was a strange mix of fear and paranoia. Over the years, most of the internal folks had been involved with at least one big project that "went south" for one reason or another. My project was unique enough that the majority of the team wanted nothing to do with it. In the minds of most, the best outcome would be that we lose the opportunity. In summary, my boss and I were having a harder time selling this opportunity to our colleagues than we were selling it to the prospect.

All of this was going on in the background while we were in a fierce fight with five of our competitors who were all bidding on this same business. In one of the most brilliant emails ever composed, we put our competition to rest in short order. And it only took one email. I state this as humbly as possible, reminding myself that anything good in me comes from God, but this email was the key to separating us from our competitors.

In the email, I simply encouraged my prospect to contact all of our competitors and ask seven key questions about them and their capabilities. I supplied answers to the questions as they related to the company that I represented. In less than a week we had signed a non-disclosure agreement, basically putting us in a position to proceed and, in effect, eliminating my competitors. The business was ours to win until we proved otherwise.

We invited our prospect to come visit our plant. When they did, our people put on a good show and presented themselves well. The manufacturing and engineering team did a great job in demonstrating our somewhat dated but still effective capabilities. The customer service team did a great job in painting the picture of an efficient and responsive team. Even the third-generation owner gave a good presentation about the history and storied past of this once very capable company. In a very short time, we were issued a purchase order for the single largest order of my career, and easily one of the top five largest orders in the history of the company. It would be the last time that we worked together on the project as a team. From that day forward, almost every person involved in that weeks-long effort to get the order retreated from that project like rats escaping from a sinking ship.

To this day, I have a hard time explaining the emotions of landing a huge new account, and then realizing that I was one of just a very few people enthused about the opportunity. The ultimate challenge for me would be slaying this dragon on my own as the guy that I reported to—the guy who supported me from day one and helped to close the order—announced that he was leaving the company. I could not and would never second-guess his decision, but his job had become a kind of living hell as his wife was dealing with some very serious health issues. Now he had an opportunity to get off the road and work closer to home. Despite my feeling that I was a man alone on an island, I was determined to press on to the point of flying solo if that is what it took to see this project to its completion.

What followed was months of encouraging, pushing, and demanding that the team get engaged and complete the project. While we had a purchase order from the customer, it was as if most of the team took the attitude of "If we ignore it, it will go away." I must confess that during that time when encouraging turned to pushing, and pushing evolved to demanding, my attitude toward many of the internal team members was not good—and that is to put it mildly! For better or for worse, anyone who knows me knows that failure is not an option.

Finally, after months of hard work and frustration, we started delivering the finished product. Thankfully, our customer was as patient as any I have ever worked with. As this huge order started to emerge like a trickle from a faucet, we started on delivering a huge order, four pieces per week out of eighty in total, literally at a snail's pace. Any other customer would have had my head on a platter, but I am eternally grateful that this particular customer was unusually understanding. Looking back, I realize that our client recognized our shortcomings from day one, realized that we were the best of not many good options, and they knew long before I knew that this was going to be a long and painful process.

In the interest of being perfectly transparent, while I am not motivated by money, my second favorite part of the sales process is getting my commission check. Someone once said that money is not the most important thing in the world, but it is right up there with air! To make matters worse, human nature had crept into this equation and I had already counted these chickens before they were hatched.

The commission check never came.

PERSPECTIVE:

The world tells us this: "You work hard; you deserve to get paid." As I do many times when I feel ripped off, I form a posse around me—a group of unwitting friends who will hear my whining and complaining, and take my side, if for no other reason than to make me feel better. In this case, the posse was unified to a man. We all shared a common distain for the guy that I was battling for my well-earned, missing commission check. It bears mentioning here that, while I am not proud of this, over the years I have become an expert at forming a posse. I have this unique gift of knowing whom to call and when to do so in an effort to make me feel better. My team of "encouragers" was quick to side with me on this one, and we shared hours of conversation slinging mud at the folks who had wronged me. In the moment, this exercise feels really good but, looking back, it is not very productive.

My Bible tells me something quite different. It tells me to be very careful about money, specifically the love of money. My Bible says

> For the love of money is a root of all kinds of evil, for which some have strayed from the faith in their greediness, and pierced themselves through with many sorrows.
>
> *1 Timothy 6:10*

So the Bible does not condemn money, but certainly provides a stern warning about the *love of money*. It gets more intense, suggesting that the love of money seems to walk hand-in-hand with a person who has strayed from the faith (like when we put our faith in money rather than in God's provision) and piercing themselves through with many sorrows. Ouch—the piercing really hurts! So while I am on record as not being motivated by money, this passage has my attention. Just for good measure, I strongly recommend a detailed study on 1 Timothy 5 and 6; these chapters cover a lot of ground on the subject of work, contentment, and idle babblings. In retrospect, I wish that I had committed some of these biblical principles to memory before I engaged in a battle over money.

Again, looking back, this situation gets worse for me, as I was in a battle over something that was not even mine! The teaching of Matthew 21:33–43 is a lesson for everyone to remember that anything and everything that we have (or think we should have) is provided by God. It does not belong to us. Verse 33 specifically states what belongs to God and what our position is: *Hear another parable: There was a certain landowner who planted a vineyard and set a hedge around it, dug a winepress in it and built a tower. And he leased it to vinedressers and went into a far country.*

Here is my paraphrase; the Landowner (God) planted a vineyard. He put a wall around it, dug a winepress, and built a watchtower. It sounds to me like a very nice, secure place. Then he rented the place to some farmers (us) and He—God—moved to another place. In summary, God provided this wonderful place and asked some people to take care of it—to manage it, if you will.

In my case, God provided a wonderful prospect in a really nice place and asked me to take care of it. To be clear, it was never mine; it was always His, and all I needed to do was take care of it. It raises the question: At what point did I think that I owned it?

In the parable, the farmers wanted to do more than just *manage* the vineyard. They got greedy and did things that that would put them in more of an *ownership* position. Here is how the story ends:

> "Therefore, when the owner of the vineyard comes, what will he do to those vinedressers?"

They said to Him, "He will destroy those wicked men miserably, and lease his vineyard to other vine-dressers who will render to him the fruits in their seasons."
Matthew 21:40–41

Again, this is another clear and present reminder to me that I am the owner of nothing; rather, I am just the manager of all that God provides for me to be over.

On the subject of money, let me end right where this chapter began in Matthew's Gospel.

For what profit is it to a man if he gains the whole world, and loses his own soul? Or what will a man give in exchange for his soul?
Matthew 16:26

In context, this passage reminds us of a few things:

- v. 24: If we desire to follow Jesus, we need to deny ourselves.
- v. 25: If I am trying to save my own life, I will lose it, but if I lose my life for Jesus, I will find life.
- v. 27: My rewards are coming later—not on earth but in heaven.

And finally, I learn in lots of different ways that by far my best source of information comes from God's Word. However, from time to time, God's Word is channeled through music. To that end, I strongly recommend Toby Mac's *Lose my Soul*. And if your playlist does not include Toby Mac, even the O'Jays (1973) knew that the love of money, money money, that "mean green," could drive some people out of their minds!

APPLICATION:

Nothing that I have is mine; I am just a manager of what God provides.

☒

Terminated, Canned; You're Fired

"I'm promoting you vertically downward."

*Do not lay up for yourselves treasures on earth, where moth
and rust destroy and where thieves break in and steal; but lay
up for yourselves treasures in heaven, where neither moth nor
rust destroys and where thieves do not break in and steal. For
where your treasure is, there your heart will be also.*

Matthew 6:19–21

• • • • • • • • • • • •

It's about a seven-hour drive from my home office in north-eastern Pennsylvania to my big, new customer's plant in northwestern Ohio. I would normally start out on a Sunday evening, drive to eastern Ohio, grab a hotel in Cleveland, and start my week early in eastern Ohio on Monday and then work my way west, calling on customers through the week before finally driving back on Friday. On this particular week, the first week of November, I made some adjustments to the trip. I worked in my office in Pennsylvania on Monday, then drove straight to western Ohio on Tuesday for an all-day meeting scheduled for Wednesday with my new customer. It would not be the most efficient trip, but things were really heating up with the new project. I had lots of issues to deal with, and there was a real possibility that I would need more than one day with my new customer.

Frankly, the Sunday-evening departures were wearing thin and I knew I was headed into trouble with some "detail" issues at my customer's plant, so I wanted to be laser focused on the task at hand and not be distracted with other customer meetings on this trip. Incidentally, in my world this was very unusual. The folks that I reported to were tracking every sales call, email, hotel stay, and meal receipt for the entire sales force. As a company, our sales were—and had been—down for some time, and the shortsighted solution from management was to whip the sales dogs harder. Surely management assumed that more sales calls and hotel stays would cure the issue of the lack of sales. The reality was that I was tired of the whipping and to a certain degree I didn't care. The new piece of business in my territory put me in "rare air" and I was projected to exceed my sales budget for the year by a wide margin. I was operating for a very short time with a kind of "Go ahead, make my day" swagger. Little did I know how short-lived this new attitude would last.

If you have never made the drive across the state of Pennsylvania on Route 80 to Ohio, let me paint the picture in three words: *long, boring* and on this particular Tuesday, *gray*. Well, at least it was not raining. About halfway through the drive, I got an email from our VP of Sales—not my boss, but his boss—telling me that I needed to be at our home office in Charlotte, NC, at 9 a.m. that Friday. This boring drive had just gotten very interesting.

There was very little doubt in my mind what this meant but I still started my last-ditch effort to keep my job. Before turning the car back east, I called my boss to let him know that being in Charlotte on Friday would be impossible as I had important meetings scheduled in Ohio for Wednesday and Thursday. He didn't pick up his phone (and that was no surprise as he was new to the company and found himself in the middle of a terrible situation) so I left a message. After a few minutes I called the VP. He, too, didn't pick up (again, no surprise, as he didn't have the guts to talk with me). So I left a message for him. And I had no choice but to call my customer, cancel my Ohio meeting, and drive back to my home office in Pennsylvania to make last-minute travel plans to fly to Charlotte for my 9 a.m. Friday meeting.

At this point, my mind was racing. I was 99 percent sure that I was getting canned on Friday, but there was this glimmer of hope that somehow we could still work this out. I had to prepare for both scenarios, but the first order of business was to call my wife, Rosemary, and let her know that I was headed back home—and why. As I knew she would be, she was completely supportive, and for that I will be forever grateful. The last thing I needed right now was to have her hammer me for losing another job. (If I haven't mentioned it, I have had more than my share of jobs over the course of my career. This book is not long enough to explain why, but, trust me, my résumé is longer than most.) I can say, without fail and to a fault, that Rosemary has never played the "Maybe you wouldn't have been fired, if you hadn't (fill in the blank)" card.

So I fly to Charlotte on Thursday night, I go to the office for my 9 a.m. Friday meeting, and by 9:20 a.m. it's over. There is no discussion about working this out—only some flimsy reason for my termination—and it's all over. To add insult to injury, my now former employer has kicked me to the curb and kicked me hard. No severance pay, no pay for unused vacation, no thanks for my service, and the healthcare benefits for me and my wife expire at the end of that day. There's a COBRA option to pay for health care at $3,700 per month, but obviously we don't exercise that option.

If you have never lost a job, congratulations; I hope you never do! But if you have lost one, and specifically, if you have been terminated, you know the range of emotions. First for me is this sense of short-lived relief, the "Thank goodness that is over" moment! For months leading up to my termination, the job had become a living nightmare so there was a sense of relief. Second, came the details of how to address the health insurance issue, filing for unemployment, updating my résumé, and mapping out a plan on what to do next. I haven't mentioned it yet—I am sixty-one years old and the prospects of landing a job at this age are not a little daunting.

All of this took some time and led us into a previously arranged ten-day trip to Israel in November. If you have never been there, I highly recommend it. This was our second trip to Israel, and it was every bit as good as the first, and in some ways better, as we traveled with our pastor and his wife. We were blessed in every way and it is a trip that we will never forget.

One final thought on the issue of losing a job: I would be lying if I didn't admit that somewhere in the range of emotions outlined above are the issues of the "What if?" and the "Why me?" questions that invariably ran through my head from time to time. While I could always come back to the fact that God knew everything that I was going through and that none of this was a surprise to Him, at the very least I found myself comparing my situation to that of others who lose their jobs. For example, union members that lose jobs have representatives who defend them and fight on their behalf; most professional athletes who lose their jobs have large, guaranteed contracts to provide a soft landing, and big-time media personalities who lose their jobs, perhaps due to some indiscretion, get the balance of their contracts paid on the way out the door. And CEOs of major corporations walk away from their positions with more money than ten families earn in a lifetime when they get canned. The reality that I had been offered nothing for my service and efforts bothered me—and it hurt.

Upon our return to the States from our Israel trip, November rolled into December and by mid-December I had reached a breaking point of sorts. The job search had turned up nothing. To make it worse, I did have some leads and a few interviews, and it became painfully obvious to me that for a number of reasons this was going to take some time or, perhaps, I may not get another full-time job. My age and the length of my résumé was working against me.

My position remains that I want to go back to work full-time, as I am healthy, able, and I think I can still bring value to an employer. Rosemary, on the other hand (and I totally respect her opinion), is leaning toward me just retiring. The problem of retiring now is addressing the health insurance issue and the fact that I am not ready to just "shut it down." If nothing else, I am a worker bee and I need to be active and productive. While we have not resolved these issues yet, we take comfort in knowing that God has a plan for us and we will follow His lead.

PERSPECTIVE:

In times of difficulty, it is very easy for me to lose perspective regarding the vast differences between my current temporary residence and my future eternal home. I dare to say that I think that many people share this difficulty. In my circle of friends, family, and associates, most of the folks that I rub shoulders with are fully consumed by the here and now. It is the exceptional person that is able to keep the challenges of this present life in perspective as compared to what awaits us in the next.

In my particular situation, I had made a couple of critical misjudgments. First I was momentarily distracted—possibly consumed—with my treasures on earth.

> Do not lay up for yourselves treasures on earth, where moth and rust destroy and where thieves break in and steal; but lay up for yourselves treasures in heaven, where neither moth nor rust destroys and where thieves do not break in and steal. For where your treasure is, there your heart will be also.
>
> *Matthew 6:19–21*

The passage above clearly tells me about my earthly treasures. In this case I don't know if it was a moth or rust or a thief (I think at one point I called my employers thieves!) but my earthly treasures vaporized before I even had a chance to touch them. In addition to the biblical instruction, our modern society warns us that we can't take our wealth with us, so I am not sure what I was thinking. More concerning to me was the realization that where my treasure was, that was where my heart was. Translated, my heart was with the earthly rewards when it should have been on helping my customers and my employers in any way possible—and that was a very sobering, convicting thought.

APPLICATAION:

Remember this is not heaven; this is earth.

The Reality of "What Next": Instacart?

"I fondly remember the time before the money ran out."

The young lions lack and suffer hunger;
But those who seek the Lord shall not lack any good thing.

Psalm 34:10

• • • • • • • • • •

At the risk of being verbally redundant, this was not the first time in my life that I found myself without a job, without the income, and without related benefits. Maybe it's a genetic thing, as my father had more than the average number of jobs over the years and there is early evidence that I may have passed the "multiple job" gene to my son. So far, no one on our family tree has worked somewhere for forty years, retired, and got the much-coveted gold watch. I actually think that our family is just slightly ahead of our time; thinking more broadly, I think that loyalty and longevity between both employee and employer is becoming a thing of the past.

But this time, something felt different; the reality of my age and the length of my résumé were clearly playing a part in my job search. I was applying for positions at 8 a.m. and getting regret emails by 4:45 p.m.

Two months passed, four months passed, and now, by mid-December, my mind was working overtime. The "stinking thinking" started to occupy too much space between my ears. There were real-life issues that needed to be addressed. We are a two-income family, so there was an economic reality in play. Thanks to my checkered résumé, my wife and I are experts at the exercise of going from two incomes to one. Rosemary is more the expert at laser sharpening a household budget and she does this from the obvious: no dining out, no more daily visits from the Amazon delivery truck (Amazon stock dropped significantly after I lost my job!), no more driving on the toll road to visit our grandkids (really, it cost more than ten dollars on the round trip!), shop around for fuel prices rather than just pulling into just any gas station, XM radio gone, and considering the removal of the sacred cow of all family budget-cutting exercises—cable TV. That last budget item is still up for debate and maybe quite soon I am going to be searching our attic for the rabbit ears antennae.

Our new budget also included the not-so-obvious things; scouring the house for "stuff" that had accumulated over the years that was no longer of use. Until recently, we had a big house and lots of stuff that had lost its purpose. So Rosemary went to work on the Facebook Marketplace and many of these items vanished and were replaced by dollars in our checking account. In the interest of total transparency, because I am the only person in America not on Facebook, I have to admit that I have no idea where the Facebook Marketplace is, but I am very thankful that it exists!

And then there was the biggest budget issue that had to be addressed: health insurance. A little earlier, I gave you the number on the COBRA option ($3,700 per month), and this was out of the question. Our only other viable option was the healthcare marketplace and that monthly premium was about $1,500 for an absolutely horrible plan with a $15,000 deductible. That is not healthcare insurance; that is larceny. So, out of necessity, we decided that we would basically "self-insure" (and by the way, this is not a recommendation) until our situation changes. We added $7,900 to our health savings account, the maximum allowed by the IRS, to an existing balance. In summary, we had about $20,000 in that account to cover medical expenses. Right out of the gate we realized savings on our prescription medicines. Again I must emphasize that we are two relatively healthy sixty-one-year-olds. Out-of-pocket prescriptions with our previous insurance was about $130 monthly; out-of-pocket without insurance and a discount card, it came to $75. A doctor's office visit with insurance resulted in a $260 bill sent to the insurance company. An office visit paid out of pocket for us came to $26. I won't bore you with more details, but in every case, including having blood work, stress test, and X-rays, it worked out exponentially less expensive when paying out of pocket the day of the service. Unfortunately, our situation is out of necessity.

If you have ever been in this position, you know that you come to a point, after you have squeezed every penny out of your budget, that there is most times "more month left at the end of the money." In mid-December we were close enough to that point that I needed to do something. A full-time job had not materialized, it was certain that no one was going to hire me during the upcoming Christmas holiday season, and three very warm coals in my potential employment fire went cold. In fact, more specifically, they went out.

I started to explore part-time independent work, a gig job as they call it. I wanted something that I could do on my schedule so that I could continue to look for full-time work and pivot quickly if something permanent came up. Uber, with all due respect, no thanks. I am weird enough, so the prospect of driving around in my car with someone potentially weirder than I am seemed scary. I tried to catch on with Postmates, but for whatever reason after repeated attempts to get signed up, I could never get past the background check. I did get a very nice thermal bag from Postmates; I hope they are not expecting me to return it! I applied at Doordash and they responded very kindly, saying something like, "We do not need any Doordashers in your area right now."

Can you sense my frustration? I was starting to think, "What is wrong with me?"

It was time to form a small posse, so I started with Tim, a friend from St. Louis. He has always been a good listener and he is never at a loss for words on a potential solution. I call Tim and share every sordid detail and frustration over my inability to get a job that any teenager with a car can get.

After listening intently, Tim fires back with the solution. "How about your local supermarket?"

What about my local supermarket? I have no idea what he is talking about. As we banter back and forth, Tim suggests that I should shop for and deliver groceries for other people. While Tim is short on details, as he many times is, the concept seems good. How hard could this be?

I head out to my local Wegmans supermarket and there it is—the answer to my gig job question is Instacart. I pick up the one-page flyer at the store and go back home to apply online and, by the miracle of smart phone technology (and the grace of God), in a matter of two days I am approved and ready to go! As I head out the door to shop my first order, Rosemary raises all kinds of negative questions. Is this safe? Will you have to deliver in bad neighborhoods? How much money are you really going to make? What about the wear and tear on our vehicle? And the most concerning of all questions: What do you know about grocery shopping?

While I was mildly disappointed with her lack of enthusiasm, I was pressing on. The truth is that she had me on the last question. I don't know a butternut squash from a banana. I don't know Quaker Oats Squares from Hollywood Squares. And the "Nature's Marketplace" section (the health food section), forget it, I was going to be totally overmatched!

So I hate to admit it but my wife was right; there was more to this grocery shopping thing than I realized, and at times I would be totally lost. It didn't help that the Instacart folks timed me, and my times were very unimpressive. Moreover, they let me know about it. But through it all, I improved and, for a high percentage of the time, my customers were happy with the service that I was providing. The fact is that they were very happy. I might have been slow, but I was accurate. At a *very* minimum, people are happy when you bring food to their doorstep, and when you bring all the *right* items to their doorstep, they are really happy.

PERSPECTIVE:

Mid-December was one of those backed-into-a-corner points in my life. I have been there a few times before; and I trust that you have been as well. Historically, my first course of action is to try to fight my way out of the corner. Eventually I run out of fight and human ingenuity, and get to a point where I call out to the One that I should have reached out to from the very beginning.

> The young lions lack and suffer hunger;
> But those who seek the LORD shall not lack any good thing.
>
> *Psalm 34:10*

Psalm 34:10 states it best. The notes in my study Bible put it this way: "People who live by their wits may eat as infrequently as young lions." By contrast those who seek the Lord shall not lack for anything.

I spent months looking for a solution, stalking like a young lion looking for a job, searching for a solution. The fact is, I was relying way too much on my own wits and not really seeking the Lord. While the Instacart situation didn't change my life, it opened my eyes to some basic realities of life, and turned my attention back to the Lord, the provider of everything that we need.

Lastly, on the subject of self-reliance versus relying on the God who created me and everything around me, I remember how a mentor of mine gave me some great advice almost thirty years ago. My mentor advised that in times of struggle, I should read the Psalms. He added specifically that "there is victory in the Psalms." That is as true in my life today as it was thirty years ago. If you do not read your Bible regularly or if you have not opened it recently, my encouragement is for you to start in the book of Psalms. There are 150 of them, and each and every chapter you read will encourage, bless, and challenge you.

And speaking of challenges, I would challenge you to start reading and show me anybody's current life situation that is not addressed in the book of Psalms. These songs that were inspired by the Holy Spirit and written by men long ago are as relevant today as they were when they were written.

APPLICATION:

....

*There are times in life when we get backed so far into a cor-
ner that there is only one way out.*

⌀

The Beauty of Simplicity

"When you put it like that, it makes complete sense."

The Lord preserves the simple;
I was brought low, and He saved me.

Psalm 116:6

● ● ● ● ● ● ● ● ● ●

Not to boast, but before too long I find my shopping skills have improved. I have changed my mode of operation from shopping multiple stores in my area to focusing on one primary store as to avoid the "jack of all trades and master of none" problem. I can say with some degree of confidence that I know more about my local Wegmans store than some people who work there.

As previously stated, I am somewhere between very organized and OCD. This character trait has also served me well in my new venture. My Instacart customers are not only getting world class service, but they are getting their cold stuff delivered cold (that's the effective use of thermal bags while shopping), their bread and bakery items delivered undamaged (the two-liter bottle of Coke is not on top of the bread), and, like a man on a mission, I am hunting down those hard-to-find "Nature's Marketplace" and "International Food" items! In summary, I am taking this new "job" seriously and, to be perfectly transparent, I am really enjoying it.

My wife and those close to me have observed my commitment to this new job and with good reason: they have questioned the entire effort. They have some good and quite reasonable questions, starting with the fact that this effort is only marginally profitable. My payment for shopping and delivering a grocery batch is between a minimum of $7 to a high of $45. Obviously, I have learned to pass on the lower-paying batches and drifted to the higher-paying batches. It bears mentioning that I am in competition with many other Instacart shoppers in my area, and we are all gunning for the higher-paying batches. While I haven't perfected the art of snagging the higher-paying batches, I have gotten pretty good at grabbing the best orders first. It's an acquired skill that requires one to stare intently at one's smart phone, watch all batches that pop up, and then make a snap decision as to which one to take. By the way, it's not as simple as it sounds; sometimes a $45 dollar order can be a loser. That $45 dollar order can be more than one order requiring me to shop multiple orders and deliver to multiple locations, so I can assure you that, even with all of my organizational skills, this is not for me. This type of multiple order brings a level of stress that I am not interested in.

A secondary concern from my well-meaning inner circle of advisers was the issue of using my vehicle to deliver the orders. I am shopping and delivering on average four orders per day. I am consuming a fair amount of fuel, and putting some significant wear and tear on the car. Notice I mentioned "the car." Early on in the process, I convinced Rosemary that I should use *her* car for this operation. My rationale was that her car was "more convenient" being a small SUV with a back hatch that was much easier to access with groceries than my sedan with a traditional trunk. She reluctantly agreed and watched each day as I proceeded to put a daily beating on her car the likes of which it had never seen before. The constant stopping and starting on the grocery runs to individual residences and the added brutality of our terrible Pennsylvania potholes on the wintertime roads took a toll on the car. The final indignity was the day that I ran into the guy in front of me while I was distracted looking at my phone trying to "snag" the next order. This little fender bender turned into a $2,000 repair. While I only had to pay the $500 insurance deductible, you can see that the Instacart profit-and-loss proposition is potentially flawed at best. Just for good measure, the guy that I ran into was even less understanding than my wife.

I assume that you are asking the obvious question:

Why would you do this? The answer is *simple*. This job of shopping for and delivering groceries to people was simple and, of all the things that I needed at this time in my life, I needed something simple. My Instacart work world consisted of three things: my smart phone, my wife's car, and a shopping cart. Simple, simple, simple, simple; did I mention simple? After working for forty-four years in every job imaginable, I finally found a job that was simple. It bears mentioning that, as my career progressed, my jobs become more complicated—more rewarding in some ways, but exponentially more complicated. I had just come out of a very complicated work situation, so this made the Instacart opportunity even more appealing.

Right behind simplicity, I was enamored by the fact that this job "worked." The phone app blew my mind. A list of items was sent to me, I pressed a button that directed me to the store, I shopped for the items, and then I pressed a button that directed me to the customer's house. The app knew everything; I needed to know nothing. I had no boss, there was no paperwork, no budgets, no sales meetings, no quality issues, no late deliveries, no unreasonable demanding customers from a certain area in my territory (and which will remain nameless because I want people from Long Island to buy my book), and did I mention this— no bosses!

And here is the kicker: I was ten times happier busting my butt and killing my wife's car to earn $400 a week than I had ever been at my former six-figure-a-year job! I can't fully explain it, but I can tell you it was for real.

PERSPECTIVE:

Before Instacart, my life at work had basically spun off its axis. Because of my nature, I was certainly part of the problem. Temperamentally, I invest too much of myself into any job and I am continually trying to improve in that area. Someday soon, God will resolve this issue once and for all and take me home to heaven. And in the meantime, my prayer is that I will achieve a better work-life balance before He takes me home.

While my suffering at work pales in comparison with what the psalmist records in Psalm 116, I love the psalm and can relate so well to it. Verses 1–9 are below for context.

I love the LORD, because He has heard
My voice and my supplications.
Because He has inclined His ear to me,
Therefore I will call upon Him as long as I live.
The pains of death surrounded me,
And the pangs of Sheol laid hold of me;
I found trouble and sorrow.
Then I called upon the name of the LORD:
"O LORD, I implore You, deliver my soul!"
Gracious is the LORD, and righteous;
Yes, our God is merciful.
The Lord preserves the simple;
I was brought low, and He saved me.
Return to your rest, O my soul,
For the LORD has dealt bountifully with you.
For You have delivered my soul from death,
My eyes from tears,
And my feet from falling.
I will walk before the LORD
In the land of the living.

Psalm 116:1–9

Verses 1–2 remind me that I can call Him at any time and that He hears me. And He not only hears me, but He inclines His ear to hear me; He is listening to hear from me! The folks that I had previously worked for weren't listening for me; my messages went straight to their voicemail.

Verses 3–4 line out some serious suffering and a call for help. I don't want to be too dramatic, but I was suffering, certainly not to the degree that the psalmist describes, but suffering nevertheless. Just to keep things in perspective, my Nelson Study Bible tells me that this psalm was most likely recited by Jesus on the night of His arrest, so my struggles cannot even begin to be compared.

In my mind, verses 5 and particularly 6 are speaking to me. *The LORD preserves the simple.* I am a simple person; I count the Instacart opportunity as a simple thing. I believe that God wants things to be simple for us; and by contrast I don't think God likes complicated things for us.

Verses 7–9 line out some of that victory in the Psalms that I mentioned earlier. All of this victory seems to be promised to the "simple." In my world, simplicity brought tremendous relief and victory.

APPLICATION:

*Some of the most beautiful things in life are the most simple.
Have you discovered this?*

Are You My Customer?

"Your promotion follows the Peter Principle. When Peter likes you, you get promoted."

By this all will know that you are My disciples, if you have love for one another.

John 13:35

• • • • • • • • • •

My two grandkids are now ten and twelve years old. They are long past the days that I would read a book to them before bedtime. My wife had purchased enough books to read to an army of children for years on end, so to say that I remember every book would be a stretch. But I do remember one called *Are You My Mother?* and vaguely recollect some story about a mother bird and baby bird somehow getting separated, leaving the baby to search high and low asking the question of many other species, "Are you my mother?"

I kind of felt that way about my new Instacart position. I take an order, I get a list and the first name and address of the person that I am shopping for, and I start shopping for essential grocery items for this person—someone I know nothing about. Right out of the gate this seemed odd to me. In every other sales or service position that I have had over the past thirty-five years, I have always known something about my customer or prospect before I have ever taken an order. I mentioned earlier that my favorite part of the sales process was the hunt; a big part of the hunt is learning as much about your customer as possible, long before you might ever get an order. In my experience, the more I know about my customer before I make contact, the better my chances of success. In the case of Instacart, there is no hunt; in fact, it is quite the opposite. I became more the hunted than the hunter, reduced to sitting in my car in the grocery store parking lot staring at my smart phone waiting to snag an order a split second before the other shoppers that I was competing with.

From my very first order, I started this little mental profiling head game trying to guess who it was I might be shopping for based on the items on the grocery list. Sometimes it was easy: diapers, baby food, formula—probably a young family. Cheerios, high-protein nutritional drinks, a shower cap, lots of notes on the list overstating the obvious ("Watch the expiration dates on the bread. . .") and adult undergarments—probably a senior citizen. And maybe the easiest one that I have had to date, the shortest list I have ever shopped, two items; a 64 oz. bottle of prune juice and a bag of organic chia seeds. I rang the doorbell upon arriving at the customer's home and was promptly greeted by a very large, middle-aged woman, who, in my estimation, looked to be very constipated. I handed off the order, got back in my car, and drove away as quickly as possible to avoid what I was positive would be an impending and potentially life-threatening explosion!

After delivering hundreds of orders, I can tell you that I am only moderately successful at pre-profiling my customers based on their grocery list. Conversely, I found it possible to learn volumes of information about a person in a very short interaction when delivering the order. Sometimes there was zero interaction when the customer instructed you to "Leave the order at the door." At first this bothered me as I had this desire to put a face with the order. Just leaving the order at the door was a bit of a disappointment. But on the flipside, wouldn't you want to meet the person that just shopped for some of your most personal items? Pre-Covid 19, most customers would greet me at the door for that less-than-five-minute exchange of groceries and pleasantries.

It bears mentioning here that I am a people person by nature and I really enjoy the short interaction at the point of delivery. I really did want to do more than just "deliver the groceries." As I mentioned before, most people are really happy to see the guy who is bringing them food, and I am, almost without exception, happy to see them. In my mind people are interesting, if nothing else.

In the pages following are some short accounts of what I found upon delivering and the people I met. First there was no rhyme or reason to connect what kind of people I was delivering to; rich people, poor people, big people, small people, old people, young people, male and female, and every race, color, and creed under the sun. It was a chance to meet new people every day! I am amazed at what you can learn about people in five minutes; their stories are a constant reminder to me of how God created us to be so unique, and yet in some ways so much the same.

Recovering Patient(s) on River Road in Wilkes Barre

. . .our roles could have easily been swapped. . .

Other than the delivery location, there didn't seem to be much out of the ordinary about this order—thirty items or so to be delivered to a man on River Road. I have lived in northeastern Pennsylvania for fifteen years and our home was located on nine acres in a wooded remote area about ten miles outside of the city of Wilkes Barre. Wilkes Barre is a typical semi-depressed northeastern Pennsylvania small city that, in some ways, time seems to have passed by. I don't know the area well enough to say for sure, but I think that the city was more prosperous during the days of coal mining. In short, I didn't spend a lot of time in the city and I had pretty much formed a negative opinion about it; but this particular home changed my opinion of the city. The home that I delivered to was old—really old—and was big and stately. It was the kind of home that you could never build today. It was a single-family home on a tree-lined street where the homes were really close together, each separated from the other by a driveway just wide enough for one car to access a garage at the rear of the home.

Upon my arrival, my customer asked me to bring the groceries inside to his kitchen and put them on the kitchen table. The multiple trips from the front entrance to the back kitchen gave me a chance to get a glimpse of the home's interior. It was kind of dark, but everything was rock solid and impressive, a place that brought to mind a time when things were built to last. For the record, entering a customer's home was a bit unusual and not really encouraged by the company management.

After I had completed the delivery, the customer thanked me and explained that we, (I assume he was referring to himself and his wife whom I didn't meet) were both recovering from recent surgeries, his being a major open-heart operation. Neither of them could get out to shop and both were instructed not to do any lifting. He gave me a $5 tip on top of the Instacart payment.

A few things dawned on me in those scant, short minutes. First, I estimate that this man was a few years younger than me. I have never had a surgery in my life, and our roles could have easily been swapped. Second, I learned something about the city that I had prejudged; there were some beautiful people and beautiful homes in the city that I considered semi-depressed.

The Mansion on the Hill

. . .my assumptions were instantly debunked. . .

It was Friday morning, late December around 11 a.m.; I was sitting in my car... waiting for an order. I had long since completed a small order earlier in the day—a not-very-profitable $17 order—and I had been sitting at least ninety minutes waiting for my next assignment. On this job, if you are not shopping, you are not earning. This is not an hourly-paid or salaried position; you are paid by the job, and this was looking to be an unprofitable day.

Boom, then it hit, a $47 job flashed on the screen of my smart phone. I snagged it before any of the other shoppers could get it. When I got inside the store and started to review the list, I could see it was long—just over 100 items, in fact—so this was going to test me at every level. I was still a bit of a rookie shopper and this list touched every base in the store: paper products to baby food; Nature's Marketplace to International Foods; deli meats to dairy; and all points in between! At some point after shopping for over two-and-a-half hours, I got a chat message from the Instacart home office alerting me to the fact that it was taking me a long time to complete this order; was there an issue? Of course there was issue. This was a huge order and as a rookie shopper I was in the deep end of the pool!

After completing the order, I hopped in my car, I hit the navigate prompt to take me to my customer's home, and I was relieved to find that the destination was only about eight miles away. At least I didn't have to drive too far to make the delivery. As I got close to the address, I pulled into a subdivision of absolutely huge, beautiful homes. I started panicking, making assumptions about whom I was delivering to. In my mind I was thinking something like this: "Huge order (over $450), beautiful home, so surely this must be the home of some rich, snooty person who at the very least is going to read me the riot act about taking so long to deliver the order. . ." Much to my relief, the homeowner did not greet me at the door. In fact, I am quite certain I was met by a hired hand, perhaps a nanny or housekeeper. She directed me to the garage where she and I proceeded to unload this massive haul of groceries. There really wasn't too much interaction between her and me—just delivering the groceries.

As we unloaded the last bags, a very pleasant woman appeared from the house, greeted me by my name, thanked me for delivering the order, and handed me an additional $20 tip. My assumptions about the snooty homeowner were instantly debunked and that $20 tip felt better than a $2,000 monthly commission check that I used to earn in my real job. By God's providence, I got that same customer order for three of the next four Fridays (the odds of that happening are astronomical), and at one point the customer asked me if she could specifically request me to shop her order. I don't know if you can appreciate how important this was to a guy that had recently been kicked to the career curb, and kicked hard. This was huge.

The Woman
Behind Moe's

*. . . she taught me more about grace, humility,
and perseverance than I might learn listening to a hundred
sermons. . .*

On this particular order, I made a mistake that I hope I never repeat. In my haste to snag the order, I missed the detail that I had just committed to shop and deliver *two* orders. This adds a level of complexity and stress that I had not signed up for. Remember, I love the simplicity of this job. I was mildly stressed.

I battled through the challenges of shopping for two orders at a time, keeping order "A" separate from order "B" in the shopping cart, going through the checkout station, loading goods in the car, and finally managing to the point of completing the first delivery. I had kept everything straight through the entire process and was now headed to the last step of an unprofitable order—delivering order "B." As I navigated to the second address, I realized that this home was in a small cluster of townhomes and apartments right behind Moe's Southwest Grill, a favorite dining spot for me and Rosemary to eat. (Did I mention that my wife and I are simple people?)

This multiple order took too long to shop and deliver, and was not very profitable for me. I was feeling a little depressed as I gathered the first few bags to be delivered from the car and approached the home. Before I could reach for the bell, a woman's voice called from inside instructing me to "Come in, William."

I often find entering people's homes a bit unusual; I step inside and there she is, Debra, sitting on her sofa, watching the Fox News Channel. But something is not right. Either she is sitting cross-legged on the sofa or she has no legs. On my second trip inside (and at the risk of staring), I steal a second glance. I am 95 percent sure she has no legs. For some reason, this freaks me out at the very least! She is having me drop the groceries right inside the door, but how is she going to get them to the kitchen? On the third and final trip inside, I ask if I can help by taking the groceries to the kitchen. Without missing a beat, and with as positive an attitude as anyone I have ever met, she says, "Oh no, I can do it; I will just take my time. I have all day."

I got back in my vehicle and had an immediate talk with myself. Here I was feeling sorry for myself because the order that I was delivering was a borderline waste of time or, at the very least, unprofitable, and I had found myself delivering to a person who had a disability that I could never imagine dealing with. I was consumed with the fact that the order had taken "too long" to deliver, and yet in comparison it would take Debra "all day" to put the order away in her home. In one brief interaction, Debra taught me more about grace, humility, and perseverance than I might learn listening to a hundred sermons on those subjects.

"Dad, The Grocery Guy Is Here!"

. . . there was something refreshing about the atmosphere in this home. . .

So with the backdrop of my never really knowing whom I am shopping for, the delivery of the order usually brings the answer to that question. I don't remember the name on this particular order but I know it was a female name, so to that end I expected a woman to answer the door upon my arrival.

As I most times do, I texted the customer from my car when I arrived at the home to communicate that I would soon be at the front door. After sending the text, I grabbed the first couple of bags from this pretty large order and proceeded to the door and rang the bell.

After one ring and a second knock, the door opened and I was greeted not by a woman but a very young man—a very young boy to be specific—I would say about four years of age. It was three o'clock in the afternoon and this young guy was dressed in just his underpants and a tee shirt.

I look at him, he looks at me, and we are both equally stumped for what seems like a very long time. He is thinking, "Who is this old guy?" and I am thinking, "Where is your mom?" After a very pregnant pause, I ask the obvious question, "Is your Mom home?" This kid who surely will grow up to be a great poker player doesn't say a word and remains expressionless for several more uncomfortable seconds. Finally after what seems like an eternity, he breaks out into this huge smile and screams at the top of his lungs, "Dad, the grocery guy is here!"

Almost instantly, this young father wades through what appears to be a huge mess of toys right near the front door. He has two more kids in tow, one looking older and the other looking younger than the kid who's just answered the door, and they proceed to take the bags from me as I place them just inside the door.

A couple of things were very obvious to me from this incident: first, Mom was not home (I met her on a subsequent delivery when one of her sons darted out the door upon my arrival); and second, there was something refreshing about the atmosphere in this home. We live in a time of dos and don'ts that, in most places, include: Don't let your small child answer the door to greet the potentially creepy grocery guy. Fortunately for me, I was not robbed of the beautiful blessing of this particular family not living in fear of every little thing, and especially not being afraid of this not-so-creepy grocery guy.

My Doctor Told Me to Change My Diet

. . .her new diet includes enough fruit, vegetables, and chicken to feed a small army. . .

At one point early in my new occupation, the Instacart people sent me a promo to recommend more shoppers in my area. I would get a referral bonus after my referral had shopped a certain number of batches. The first victim was my son. He shopped his agreed-upon ten batches, and I got a $100 bonus. This was easy money, and it was at this point I found myself wishing that I had five more kids... well, too late for that.

The next promo was way more unreasonable. The incentive was $250 for something crazy like ninety batches in thirty days. Despite the unreasonable proposition, my wife signed up just to try to support me in any way that she could. Bear in mind that Rosemary is a very successful businessperson, the owner of two small businesses, so the last thing she needed was another job! If nothing else, her willingness just underscores her love for me, and, at the very least, we could maybe "double team" this thing one day a week and earn some extra cash to pay the repair bill on her car that I was systematically destroying.

On a Saturday morning, while Rosemary was not busy with her real job, we headed out to the supermarket for the first day of her third job. The plan was for me to help her with the first few orders—not that she didn't know how to shop for groceries—as the phone app was a little tricky and, that way, I could save her from learning the hard way.

The first couple of orders went pretty well. She is no stranger to the grocery store and she was doing just fine with the phone. The problem was that there weren't many orders on this particular Saturday, and we spent a long time in the car that afternoon just waiting. The only thing worse than one person sitting around waiting is two people sitting around. . .

Finally, around 4 p.m., a big order hits and my wife snags it, demonstrating some really fast fingers on the smart phone to get this order ahead of the other shoppers. This order is going to be a challenge as there are eighty-plus items, but it is a nice payout, somewhere around $40. Just as we start to shop, my phone lights up with two delivery-only orders for $27; I can't resist, so I take the orders. I can see the expression of concern on Rosemary's face as I tell her that she is on her own to shop for the big order, as I have to leave her while I deliver the two orders that I have just committed to. In my mind, the timing will be perfect. I will run off to deliver the two orders, and then circle back just in time to help her deliver the order that she is shopping for.

I pick up the two delivery-only orders and head out to complete my part of this double-team assignment. My first concern is the distance as these two orders are neither close to the pick-up point nor close to each other. My second concern is the rush-hour traffic. We do not live in a big metro area, but 5 p.m. is 5 p.m. and I find that I am not making good time. As I get back to the supermarket to pick up my wife, I am mildly concerned that she will be finished and waiting at the door for me. But as I enter the store, I don't see her. I walk past all of the checkout stations; surely she must be finishing up there, but there is no wife in sight. The frozen department—those are always the last items to shop—but no dice. . . . Where in the world is she?

Finally, I spot her in the dairy section. I have no idea how she is only in the dairy section, as that is about half way through the order. As I get closer to Rosemary, I see an expression on her face that I have only seen once or twice in the more than forty years that I have known her— somewhere between freaked out and in a total meltdown. This order has gotten the best of her. Please understand the significance: my wife is confident, capable, competitive, and sometimes cocky. She is one of those people who rarely ever lose. . .

I get an immediate rush of adrenaline. "Mr. What-Do-You-Know-About-Grocery-Shopping" is getting a chance to bail out "Mrs. I-Am-Better-Than-You-At-Most-Everything." I grab a cart and, like a knight in shining armor, I help my wife to complete the order—double time!

It's now well past 6 p.m. on this January night. We hop into the car to make the delivery of this massive haul of groceries. Even with the GPS, the customer's place is hard to find in the dark. I had never been to this part of town, and it becomes apparent that we are hopelessly lost as we meander through this low-income housing development trying to find "Building #3." As I stop at a cross street for a stop sign, Rosemary spots a big, rough looking guy standing on the corner, and before I can say, "Lock the doors," she rolls down the window and says, "Excuse me, can you tell us where Building #3 is?" Did I mention that my wife might lack some street smarts? So this guy grunts out some directions, which I am positive are going to take us to an even darker part of the neighborhood where he will rendezvous with some associates to relieve these two old people driving through their turf on a Friday night of the $400 worth of food in the car!

Much to my amazement, the directions from my wife's new friend actually lead us right to Building #3. I instruct her to stay in the car until I confirm that we are at the right building. As I enter the common area of the complex, I pick up the combined scent of cat urine and/or stale beer. Please understand that I am not judging, I am just trying to set the scene. Rosemary and I lived in places similar to this early in our marriage, so I am not "above this"—but at this time of the evening it is the kind of place that is not a little concerning.

I zero in on the exact apartment, knock on the door, and I am greeted by this very pleasant middle-aged woman in this very small apartment. I confirm that I am in the right place and, with the help of my wife, proceed to unload this huge order. Both Rosemary and I are quietly wondering what this woman is going to do with all of this food as she is clearly living alone in this small apartment. As we fill her kitchen table and every chair around the table with bags of groceries, we are joined in the small apartment by a curious neighbor who seems to have the same concern: What is all of this food for?

The neighbor addresses the elephant in the room, asking without hesitation, "What's up with all of this food?" Without missing a beat, the recipient of the food explains that she has multiple health issues and, at her doctor's urging, she is "changing her diet." I don't know what her old diet looked like but I can assure you that her new diet includes enough fruit, vegetables, and chicken to feed a small army. We may never know how this new diet worked out, but we certainly have no questions about this woman's commitment to the new program.

"Do You Do Any Driving?"

. . . she had a disproportionate growth of long facial hair even for an older lady. . .

While we don't live in a big city, there are a few high-rise complexes in Wilkes Barre, Pennsylvania, and these residences do present more of a challenge when making the actual delivery of the groceries. I haven't made many deliveries to these high-rise complexes but a very unscientific survey conducted by me indicates that many of the residents are older and less mobile, so the service I am providing is very convenient and helpful.

I am no spring chicken myself, but I have observed that people of a certain age, a few years older than me, have less of a filter and do not hesitate to ask questions or express opinions more freely.

In this incident, I found a parking spot in the city center and consolidated the eight bags of groceries to four so that I could make just one trip from the car to the second floor of my customer's building. I punched in the code I had been provided to enter the building and I decided that I would take the steps to the second floor rather than using the elevator. Half way up the steps, I recognized my miscalculation on the steps-versus-elevator decision, but I pressed on nonetheless.

I knocked on my customer's door and, after what seemed to be a long time, a very unique (in many ways) older lady answered the door. Do you remember that I mentioned earlier that I am an expert at making snap evaluations of people on my initial interaction with them?

In a word, she was eccentric, bordering on odd. She only opened the door far enough for me to hand off the bags, but from what I could see of her apartment, it appeared to be very disorganized and very overcrowded. I got the impression she might be a borderline hoarder. She was short and slight, she had a disproportionate growth of long facial hair even for an older lady, and the fashion statement that I still can't get out of my mind was the hat she wore. It was not just any hat; certainly it was a hat that was not off the shelf. This was a handmade hat, knitted or crocheted (I don't know the difference). And here is the kicker about the hat: It very much resembled the cover of a handmade spare roll of toilet paper that I remember my Aunt Ruth had in her bathroom when I was a kid. The fact that my aunt had the time and the talent to make a spare toilet paper roll cover for her bathroom amazed and amused me, but fifty years later to see what appeared to be exactly the same item on this lady's head shocked and tickled me all at the same time.

Keep in mind that all of this was happening quickly. In the middle of all of the snap profiling and visual imagery, she hit me with a crazy question that I was not anticipating. With a tiny voice, looking me straight in the eye she asked, "Excuse me, do you do any driving, and might you be able to give me a ride somewhere?" My mind was racing. I sensed a genuine need but for a multitude of reasons I had to decline, and I needed to do so fast. I respectfully declined, but I walked away from her door feeling as if I should have done more or have had a better answer.

Smoky and the Neighbor

. . . I could tell that she was far happier to give than she was to receive. . .

The Instacart app gives me a prompt when I am shopping for a customer who is new to the Instacart system. While there is no really clear reason given by the company for notifying me, I assume that they want me to know this information for one particular reason: I only get one chance to make a good first impression. As I shop this order, I am being extra careful given that this is a new customer.

I shop the order in good time and I head out to make the delivery, looking forward to meeting the lady who will soon receive her first order. It is not a particularly large order—in fact, fewer than twenty items. I have a little trouble finding her house as it is not very well marked and the place is not in great shape. Upon arrival, I text her to let her know I am in her driveway. There's no reply.

I grab a couple of bags and walk toward a screened-in porch on the side of the house. I see someone behind the screen of the porch. As I get closer, I realize that it is a man not a woman; it is one o'clock in the afternoon and this guy is sitting inside drinking a bottle of beer and smoking a cigarette. As a recovering alcoholic, I am not judging, but 1 p.m. is a bit early to be drinking. The small porch is fully engulfed with the cigarette smoke, but duty calls and I enter into this smoky enclosure. Either happy hour has started early here or, as they say, "It's five o'clock somewhere."

Still not 100 percent sure that I am at the right house, I ask the fellow if he is expecting a grocery order. In a very few words, his reply comes: "No, she is," as he nods his head toward the house. I ask if I should go in, so he nods, yes. I enter in through the kitchen and a see a lady sitting in the living room. With the aid of a walker, she gets up to greet me in the kitchen. As I deliver the packages, she tells me that she is recovering from a recent surgery and that this has been her first attempt at ordering groceries online and she is extremely pleased to see me.

She also introduces me to her neighbor, the guy drinking and smoking out on her porch. Again, in my mind I am making all kinds of judgments and assumptions. Who is this guy, and what is his relationship to the lady? If he is a friend, why doesn't he help her out by shopping for her groceries? And lastly, wouldn't it probably be better for everyone if he were in the grocery store at 1 p.m. rather than drinking on · his neighbor's porch?

So just as I am at the height of my judging and profiling, the lady warmly thanks me and hands me a $20 bill. I put up some mild resistance to accepting the money as I can clearly see that the $20 would be better in her purse than in my pocket. However, she insists, explaining that she had received a promo from Instacart and her entire first order was free, and that she would have spent far more than $20 if she had to pay for the order.

As I reflect on this now, most importantly, I could tell that she was far happier to give than she was to receive; the entire short interaction blew my mind.

"Is This 17 West Ross Street?"

. . . I was amazed at her determination and an air of contentment about this lady. . .

The thing I remember about this order was that it was easy, there weren't too many items, there were no crazy-weird items that I could not find, and there was a "heavy order" bonus for me because the order included a case of bottled water.

The challenge came on the delivery end, as I had to deliver to the city, and from the satellite image on my GPS, it looked like I was delivering to an apartment complex. I circled the city block twice before I decided to pull in to a little parking lot beside a small apartment complex that did not have a visible address on the building. I have to mention that a couple of weeks earlier, I had delivered an entire order to the wrong apartment complex, so I did not want to make the same mistake twice.

I left the order in the parked car and walked to the front of the building to try to confirm the address. In my haste, I walked right past a woman who was just standing in front of the building holding one of those canes that blind people use to survey the area in front of them as they walk.

No luck; I couldn't find any numbers on the building and I was getting concerned. But maybe the blind lady could help me. "Excuse me," I asked, "is this 17 West Ross Street?"

Without missing a beat, she replied, "Yes it is. Are you William from Instacart?"

"Yes, I am," I replied.

Forgive me again, but I was not expecting a blind person; and it's not that blind people don't need groceries, it's just that I was a bit taken aback. By the way, I could tell from our brief interaction that she was totally blind, not partly sighted yet technically or legally blind. Hers was the "feeling her way around with that cane" kind of blindness.

She suggested that I go back to the car and get the groceries and she would meet me inside the first door of the building, where she she had a cart waiting to load the groceries.

I grabbed the case of water and a couple of bags on the first trip, met her inside, and then went back for the remainder of the bags on the second trip. I now had all of this stuff inside the little entry area of the apartment complex, and the lady asked me to put it all in her cart so that she could take it to her apartment. I respectfully suggested that all of this stuff was not going to fit in her little cart. I could see it was one of those rectangular-shaped lightweight carts, tall and narrow with two large wheels that roll when you tip the cart.

"It will fit," she informed me confidently. "I have done this before." She proceeded to tell me to put the case of water in first, standing the case on its end, and then she told me how to load every other item so that each of them would fit perfectly into the cart. And keep in mind she was doing all of this without the benefit of her eyesight! By contrast, my eyesight is perfect and I could see no way that all of this stuff was going to fit into this small cart. Note to self: There is a huge difference between vision and eyesight!

After the cart was loaded, she politely but abruptly thanked me and said good-bye. "Oh no," I insisted, "I would like to help you get the order to your apartment." In my mind, I had no concept of how she would get through the next set of doors that required a pass code to be punched into a keypad, into an elevator that I could see on the other side of the secured door, and ultimately into her apartment.

"No really," she insisted, "I do this all of the time."

She was determined and I was not going to win this debate. I got back in my car, pulled out of the parking lot, and glanced back into that small entryway to see her feeling around the wall to find the keypad that would gain her entry to the main building.

I cannot explain my mixed emotions. On one hand, I wanted to go back in and insist that I should be of more assistance, but on the other hand, I was amazed at her determination and the air of contentment that this lady had and that was both admirable and very much missing from my world at that very moment. I was tortured about her situation and condition, and she was as cool as a cucumber.

This was clearly another situation that the Lord had arranged for the express purpose of having me learn something, and what I needed to learn had nothing to do with delivering the groceries.

Thinking About Instacart

"Why do you say we should go paperless?"

By this all will know that you are My disciples, if you have love for one another.

John 13:35

· · · · · · · · · ·

PERSPECTIVE:

Through all of these customer interactions, something strange or unusual was happening. I started out on this part-time job trying to make a few extra bucks, but something far bigger and different was unfolding.

First of all and as I mentioned earlier, the profits that I was netting were pretty skinny; after figuring the hours I was working, and considering the wear and tear on the car, this was not a very profitable enterprise. Second, and more important, this operation was becoming way more about the people that I was delivering to than it was about me and the money I was earning. In a high percentage of the cases, the folks that I was shopping for had a need or a situation that prevented them from shopping for a basic need—food. I was filling that need.

I am not proud of this, but I must be transparent and tell you that when I started this part-time job, my intentions were not humanitarian; my intentions were to make a few extra dollars. But here is the crazy part: I was hooked! The more I shopped, the more interactions I was having with people that had a need. The fact is I could take a lot more of your time to tell you many more stories of how I was blessed most every time that I made a delivery.

By this all will know that you are My disciples, if you have love for one another.
John 13:35

It dawned on me that I was unknowingly demonstrating the love of Christ by loving others through this simple act of shopping for them and delivering their groceries. It became more important than ever to me to not just "shop for the groceries" but to do it with a greater purpose, with an attitude of demonstrating love for others. I have to confess that in my forty years of working for a living, I had never approached my job with this attitude. Work was "work." I did it begrudgingly at times, and it was frustrating most times, really quite unfulfilling.

God was in the process of stripping me down to the very basics of the true purpose of work—serving and loving others—and it only took forty years for me to get to this point!

APPLICATION:

Don't overcomplicate what God wants you to do.

ℒ

What is
Service,
Anyway?

"Let's identify our weaknesses. . .
and don't look at me when you list them."

*Now I beg you, brethren, through the Lord Jesus Christ, and
through the love of the Spirit, that you strive together with
me in prayers to God for me, that I may be delivered from
those in Judea who do not believe, and that my service for
Jerusalem may be acceptable to the saints*

Romans 15:30–31

• • • • • • • • • • • •

Seeing that this is a book about service, now is probably a
good time to discuss service. Here is what Webster says:

*Service (noun): act or result of serving; duty performed
or needs supplied.*

The Bible has a lot to say about the word *service*. It is
mentioned 133 times. The term *servant* occurs 494 times,
servants 476 times, *serve* 209 times, and *served* 74 times.

I did a quick survey of some prominent companies and I
found the following regarding their position on the issue of
service.

Mission Statement of a US Automaker

*To earn customers for life by building brands that inspire
passion and loyalty through not only breakthrough technol-
ogies but also by serving and improving the communities in
which we live and work around the world.*

Mission Statement of an Overseas Automaker

*To attract and attain customers with high-valued products
and services and the most satisfying ownership experience
in America.*

Vision Statement:
To be the most successful and respected car company in
America.

MISSION STATEMENT OF A BANK

To offer lending and investment products that: Serve low-
and moderate-income individuals and families, improve
underserved low- and moderate-income communities, and
create sustainable practices for the long haul.

So, please pardon my skepticism but some of the above statements feel kind of cliché, almost empty regarding the issue of service. While I was on this search of what some major companies think about service, I found some mission statements brought a smile to my face as I read them. Here are a few for your review:

MISSION STATEMENT OF A BEVERAGE CO.

To refresh the world. To inspire moments of optimism and
happiness. To create value and make a difference.

(My response: I am sorry but gag me with a soda; they are providing a soft drink, not a belief system!)

MISSION STATEMENT OF A COMPUTER CO.

To bring the best user experience to its customers through its
innovative hardware, software, and services.

And in a manifesto, the CEO set the vision specified in these words:

We believe that we are on the face of the earth to make great
products, and that's not changing.

(My response: Do I detect a little "It's all about us and our greatness" in this manifesto?)

MISSION STATEMENT OF A SOFTWARE CO.

To empower every person and every organization on the planet to achieve more.

The company goes on to make the point that *empowerment* is the key idea in the mission statement, representing the primary objective of the company and what the strategic tactics of the organization are endeavoring to achieve.

(My response: It's comforting to know that when I need to be empowered, this software provider will be there for me. *Ughhh!*)

✄

These are large companies and I find their stated positions to be seemingly lacking the commitment to service. I do not think that these big companies are unique; I find many businesses large and small to be missing the mark on service.

Even more offensive to me are the folks that "talk the service talk," but who do not "walk the service walk." The company that I recently separated from was a prime example. We charged our clients a premium for our products, backed by the promise of world-class support and customer service. I am a huge proponent of this value proposition based on the simple premise that "You get what you pay for" and to pay a small premium for a product and related *services* that will improve your bottom line, you are far better with that combination of an excellent product *and* excellent service. Unfortunately, we had shifted from being a company that was known as much for its service in the past, to a company that still charged a premium but merely *talked about service rather than actually providing the service.*

SLEEPING IN COMFORT...

My wife and I recently put our money where our mouth is. After twenty years of sleeping on our early-generation Tempur-Pedic mattress, we decided it was time for a new mattress. We paid a premium twenty years ago for that mattress and it served us well but, trust me, it was time. We live in a remote area so we traveled seventy miles to Philadelphia to the King of Prussia Mall, the largest mall within 300 miles and a place where we could "test drive" every premium mattress under the sun—conveniently all in one place.

Rosemary and I tried the Sleep Number, the Casper, the Purple, the Tempur-Pedic and every other option in between in one long, grueling day. After all of the testing was done, not surprisingly we were leaning heavily towards the Tempur-Pedic. Part of that preference was based on our historically good experience with our first Terpur-Pedic and the zero-gravity setting on the adjustable base on this particular bed that spoke volumes to my then-sixty-one-year-old achy back.

But here was the problem: the price on the bed and the base was just over $6,000, or just for perspective, about the same price as our first ever brand-new car, a 1976 Olds Cutlass! The sales woman at the store did a great job of selling the value, the bed was awesome on the test drive, and the thing that might have put me over the top was the promise of a "white glove delivery." This spoke to my OCD, and, just for good measure, made me less concerned about the white carpet in our master bedroom.

On the day of the delivery, all of the talk of the "white glove delivery" went out the proverbial window. The truck was late and it was a hot day. I could sense immediately that it had been a long day for the two guys on the truck. You could feel the tension between the two of them as they debated almost every detail about how to get the mattress and the base from their truck to our bedroom. The truck, by the way, was not their truck; it was a dirty Ryder Rental truck. Right out of the gate, these guys were set up to fail. The salesperson had promised a "white glove delivery" and the delivery guys were dispatched in a dirty rental truck.

No worries; surely these guys would remove the mattress and the base from the dirty corrugated boxes *outside* of my home as to not drag the dirty boxes across the white carpet in our bedroom. . . not a chance; by then I was on a slow boil. As the delivery and assembly of the bed continued, there were several other minor issues that didn't measure up to the promise of a "white glove delivery" and, needless to say, I was feeling less than enthused about paying a premium for a service that, in reality, turned out to be less than average.

How could such a simple question regarding service get so lost in the world that we live in now? In my estimation, excellent service is a rarity today. In fact, it is so rare that when I have a great "customer experience" related to service, I am at most times surprised. In summary, excellent service is the exception, not the rule.

BETTER NEWS WITH THE CAR. . .

Speaking of exceptions, I have an example that I should share. We struggled for years to find a good, reliable service shop for our cars. I am a buy-and-hold guy when it comes to cars. I buy brand new vehicles, finance them at 0 percent for three to five years, and then drive them for three to five more years with my only expense on the back end of the life of the car being any repairs made. I am referring specifically to my 2012 Toyota Camry, the best car I have ever owned, by the way, but the brakes were giving me trouble. We were long past the initial 24,000-mile period where Toyota was doing all service at no charge in response to the unexplained rare instances when one of their products would accelerate on its own and cause injury or death. In fact, we were so well past it, that the car now has 260,000 miles clocked up on it. I tried a couple of local shops other than the dealership service department but none was able to resolve the issue. I was basically running through brakes every 20,000 miles—not good when compared to the 80,000 miles that I got out of the OEM brakes. The Toyota dealership also tried solving the problem, but the result was the same—the brakes only lasted 20,000 miles.

A good friend recommended Mike Meoni, a guy with a shop about a forty-minute drive from my home. I was advised that Mike would do two things: *first,* he would fix the problem; and *second,* he would be as expensive or slightly more so than the dealership. I talked with Mike and he assured me that he could fix the problem and that he would get paid accordingly. Mike fixed the problem, first shot out of the gate, and I had to ask what his secret was. He advised me that there was no secret to this and that his success was based mostly on a collection of what he called "little things" that he did that others before him probably had not done. He told me that he only used OEM products directly from Toyota; he told me that all of his technicians were formally trained and kept current on all new techniques through continuing certified training; and then he rattled off about six little detail things that he did as a standard practice that I am quite positive others before him had not done. These were clearly small details, but yet another example of "Simple Service" making the difference between a very frustrated customer and a satisfied customer for life. No one other than Mike will ever touch my vehicles, regardless of the price.

PERSPECTIVE:

As you have gathered from my ranting above, I believe that service is something of a lost priority. You might also have gathered how important I think service is. And, lastly, I don't feel bad about pointing out this collective blind spot in society as it has taken me forty years of working to realize the error of my ways.

> Paul, a bondservant of Jesus Christ, called to be an apostle, separated to the gospel of God.
>
> *Romans 1:1*

The apostle Paul, author of one of the most significant books of the Bible, Romans, refers to himself as a bondservant of Jesus Christ. To be clear, that word *bondservant* means *slave.* Paul is talking about a voluntary slavery undertaken out of love, not the forced slavery known to many in the Roman Empire. Paul emphasizes his personal subjection to Jesus Christ.

> Now I beg you, brethren, through the Lord Jesus Christ, and through the love of the Spirit, that you strive together with me in prayers to God for me, that I may be delivered from those in Judea who do not believe, and that my service for Jerusalem may be acceptable to the saints.
>
> *Romans 15:30–31*

Near the end of the letter to the Romans and from the passage above, Paul expresses yet again commitment to service. In the original translation this word service is *diakonia* meaning *aid, service, ministry.* This was no "deliver the groceries" service work; rather, this was "risk your life ministry on this trip to Jerusalem." Paul was clearly all in on the concept of service.

In summary, I started this chapter asking the question, "What is service?" Now, I would like to add a second question. "What has happened to service in the world we live in today?"

First, I would suggest that in today's environment, service has become a four-letter word. We talk about it, we claim to provide it, but if we read the mission statements from some of the biggest companies in the world, it's an empty promise. There are too many references to innovation, empowerment, optimism, happiness, passion, and sustainable practices. And there are too few mentions of simple service.

At a deeper and more disturbing level, I suspect that the whole idea of service or being a servant is frowned upon in today's world where people's priorities are captured in a spirit of "What can you do for me?" Dare I say that the concept of being a servant is a million miles away from today's desire for happiness, optimism, and empowerment? The reality is that we cannot offer service if we do not commit to being servants.

So, one last time, what is service? Service is ministry. Service is simple. Imagine what your work experience would look like if you had adopted this priority to serve first and let all the other "stuff" come *after* the concept of serving others first.

Imagine what our world would look like if we combined the serve-minister principle with the command to love others (as stated in the previous chapter). This simple serve-minister-love manifesto could change the world.

APPLICATION:

Don't be afraid to be a servant; just be sure that you are serving the right Master.

SERVE / MINISTER / LOVE

Gotta Serve Somebody

"Part of the problem is the number of employees
who think they know the solution."

No servant can serve two masters; for either he will hate the one and love the other, or else he will be loyal to the one and despise the other. You cannot serve God and mammon.

Luke 16:13

• • • • • • • • • •

I started my first job in May of 1969; I delivered daily newspapers, 365 days a year, for the *Philadelphia Evening Bulletin*. Every Monday through Saturday, I delivered to forty-eight individual homes, and to thirty-five homes on Sunday morning. You had to be twelve years old to get the job. I was eleven but I wanted to work so badly that I lied about my age. At the age of eleven you are old enough to deliver newspapers but you are still young enough to cry. When a dog bit me on my paper route, a huge St. Bernard, I cried like a baby! This happened within the first thirty days on the job; despite giving birth to a lifelong fear of dogs, I pressed on. I was forever scarred by the entire episode.

I was compensated handsomely making between $10–12 weekly. The pay plan, as I remember it, was 95 percent based on customer tips. The better the service, the better the tips— some things never change. I often tell people that I felt like I had more money back then than I have had at any other time in my working career. There were times during the five years that I delivered newspapers that my parents had to borrow money from me to pay our family's bills.

In addition to my getting my first job, a lot of other stuff happened in 1969. The Beatles played their last public performance on the roof of Apple Records; the Jets (yes, the Jets!) led by Joe Namath beat the Colts in Super Bowl III; the Boeing 747 made its first commercial flight; Neil Armstrong became the first man to walk on the moon; Charles Manson and a group of his disciples murdered five people in Los Angeles; Woodstock drew over 400,000 people to a music festival in New York; the Mets beat the Orioles for the World Series; and Tiny Tim married Miss Vicky on the Tonight Show hosted by Johnny Carson.

The details of the events above and many more were basically communicated in one of two ways: either a daily newspaper or three evening network television news broadcasts. That was it; there was no twenty-four-hour cable news, no Internet, no Facebook, and no cell phones. Not to be overly dramatic, but my delivering the daily newspaper was a pretty big deal. People were relying on me to deliver important information to their doorstep every day. In some ways, I was their connection to all that was happening in their neighborhood, in our country, and around the world. Even as an eleven-year-old kid, I recognized the importance of not just doing the job, but doing it in a timely and professional manner. If it was raining or windy, I put the papers inside of storm doors rather than on the doorstep. If it was snowing, we didn't get a "snow day." The papers had to be delivered.

Even back then, people appreciated exceptional service. I had one customer, Mrs. Perry from 3336 Chesterfield Road in Philadelphia, send a handwritten letter to the *Philadelphia Evening Bulletin* to express her sincere appreciation for the job that I was doing by delivering her newspaper each and every day without fail. Our local branch manager recognized me, and he read the letter to all of the other carriers before presenting the letter to me. If you are wondering how much that letter meant to me, think about the fact that I remember Mrs. Perry's address whereas I don't remember some of my own former addresses!

Fast forward to much later in life when I was in my mid-thirties and I desperately needed a career change. I had spent fifteen years working on the manufacturing side of business—specifically the business of printing labels and packaging. Without the benefit of a formal education, I worked extremely hard to progress through the internal ranks to advance myself to the position of plant manager with sixty people reporting to me. The fact is that I was in over my head, as managing sixty people was not my area of expertise. I know as much (or even more) about the printing business as anyone in my industry, but I knew nothing about the challenges of dealing with sixty personalities. I failed miserably and was unceremoniously fired.

I vowed to make a fresh start. I was finished with manufacturing, and I was going to move into sales. I ran into two problems, however: I knew nothing about sales and my job search for sales positions turned up nothing. No one was going to take a chance on hiring a manufacturing guy to do sales.

When I was almost ready to give up, a very good friend offered me a sales job. He owned a small ink manufacturing company and he needed a sales guy. The salary for the position was about one third of what I had been making in my former manufacturing job, but I did have a chance to earn additional income in the form of commissions. The job offer was conditional: I had to agree to attend some sales training sessions set up and paid for by my friend and new employer. Because I knew nothing about sales, it seemed like a reasonable condition. On the very first day of the job, my boss dispatched me to the trainer's office where I met a guy—his name was Mike—who would become a mentor and friend for life. As matters would be, unfortunately the first session did not go well.

After we had exchanged pleasantries, Mike opened the session with a seemingly simple question: "Why do you want to go into the sales profession?"

Without hesitation, I replied, "I want to make a lot of money."

After a very long pause, Mike told me that was the wrong answer, ended our session after just fifteen minutes, and told me that if I did not come back with a better answer the following day, I will never make it in sales.

I felt crushed. I had failed the first test and I found myself racking my brain for the next twenty-four hours trying to think of the correct answer. I arrived on day two with no clue as to what the right answer to the question was and I had to ask Mike to please tell me the correct answer. What Mike shared next was something that I will never forget: he told me that the most successful people in sales were the people in the profession with their primary goal being to *help others*. To be honest, helping others was the furthest thing from my mind; my primary goal was to help myself. I count Mike's advice on that day to be some of the wisest counsel I have ever received. Mike graciously allowed us to restart the training with the understanding that helping others— serving them—had to be our primary objective.

So from a very early age, and at various junctures throughout my life, I learned the value and necessity of serving people. In the interest of total transparency, I haven't always put the need to serve in its proper place on my priority list but I have always *known* the importance. In the previous chapter, we considered how the apostle Paul made serving a priority. So it raises the obvious question: Whom are you serving? Better still, are you even serving?

My apologies for the potentially offensive questions. Perhaps you may not be on board with the concept of serving. After all, just because the apostle Paul and the guy writing this book think it's a good idea, you may be thinking, "I don't see the need to serve."

The fact of the matter is you *are* serving already, even if you think you are not. Every person on the planet is serving somebody or something every day of his or her life. Some of us serve willingly, without question, and not really giving much thought to the act of serving. In most healthy families, husbands serve wives, and wives serve husbands. Parents serve children, and children serve parents. Employees serve employers. Much of this goes on every day without a lot of thought going into the service.

There is also a large measure of unhealthy service in everyday life, a darker service that drifts invariably into bondage. Some are serving alcohol, drugs, sex, money, or pornography. These, and many others, can be the cruelest of masters. During my lifetime, I have served some of those cruel masters, and I can tell you from personal experience that when you are serving the wrong master, service is anything but simple.

PERSPECTIVE:

At this point, whether you agree or not, you are going to serve somebody or something. Even people like Bob Dylan know that. Think about the lyrics of his songs, such as *Gotta Serve Somebody,* a song that starts with the words *You may be an ambassador to England or France.* You can check out the words online,1 but note how his point is that even if you are an ambassador, gambler, heavyweight champion or a bejeweled socialite, you are going to have to serve someone!

Dylan's message was proclaiming in great detail that not only will you serve somebody, but that your master will be one of two choices: either the devil or God. You may think what you want about Mr. Dylan, but for me this is another one of those instances where my playlist and the Bible agree. Here is what God's Word says.

> No servant can serve two masters; for either he will hate the one and love the other, or else he will be loyal to the one and despise the other. You cannot serve God and mammon.
>
> *Luke 16:13*

While Luke 16:13 does not line out the exact two choices that Dylan gives us, Luke is in total agreement that we can only serve one Master.

In summary, I feel like I am in good company when I suggest that *service is simple*; there are only two choices, and you are going to serve either one or the other.

---

1 See https://www.azlyrics.com/lyrics/bobdylan/gottaservesomebody.html

APPLICATION:

Make sure that you are serving the right Master.

Why Serve?

"I see we are split between those who like my tie
and those who prefer unemployment."

Just as the Son of Man did not come to be served, but to serve, and to give His life a ransom for many.

Matthew 20:28

• • • • • • • • • • •

At the age of fifteen, I picked up a habit that would take hold of my life, quickly consume me, and ultimately almost destroy me. That destructive force was alcohol. What started out as something that seemed innocent and a perfect way for an introverted kid to fit in with a group of friends progressed to an addiction that determined my every move and influenced my every decision. Alcohol was my cruel master, and I was serving that master in every aspect of my life. Alcohol was systematically destroying my marriage, my relationship with my son, my work and the relationships that I had at work, my health, and everything in between.

In an effort to save my family and my marriage, I quit drinking at the age of thirty-two. Oh I had stopped many times before, only to gradually start again after a short period of time, each time laying down some self-imposed rules ("I'll only drink on the weekends, blah, blah, blah!") in an effort to manage the beast. The theory was that I would be the master; the alcohol would be the slave. But this never works. The weekends soon started to begin on Friday, then on Thursday and they extended to Monday. If you have ever been there, you know the drill.

However, this time was different. If I am nothing else, I am determined. I quit drinking on January 1 after a New Year's Eve party at my sister's home that scared me. As the evening progressed, we made a royal mess of my sister's new home and nearly burnt the place down trying to light a fire in the fireplace. In my estimation, every person in that house was blind drunk by the end of the party. I was done; I was determined to quit.

January turned to February, then February into the early spring—and I was clean, without a drop of alcohol. At the end of May, we took our traditional Memorial Day camping trip and the first issue presented itself. That weekend, I discovered that I never really liked camping, and that what I liked was drinking. The camping trip was just an excuse to hang out with my friends and family to drink. I promise you that this never dawned on me until we were already at the campsite and by then I felt miserable. I relapsed and had a few drinks during the course of the weekend. It was horrible, and with each drink I hated myself even more so that by the end of that weekend I was in a very dark place. After the trip, I got right back on the zero-alcohol wagon, but the internal battle in my mind—the battle between the cruel master and the servant who was on the run—was maddening. As the internal struggle increased, my attitude and behavior got worse. I was impossible to live with, and I think the people who knew me best were hoping that I would just go back to drinking!

Finally, in the spring of the next year after eighteen months of madness, at the urging of some great friends and by the prompting of the Holy Spirit, I invited Christ into my heart and my life was changed forever. I did not instantaneously change from a raging madman to the best husband and father in America, but a new creation was born that day and the path to a better life was coming into focus. The cruel master was gone, and on that day, Jesus Christ became not just my Savior but also my *Lord*. From that day forward, I was serving the right Master.

As my years of sobriety added up, I never ever had a desire to take a drink. I did, however, still have some unresolved issues. After many years clean, I started attending a biblically based twelve-step recovery meeting called *Celebrate Recovery*. This group has helped me to address some of the underlying issues that I was dealing with and, believe it or not, the twelfth step is basically a call for those who have been helped by the program to share what they have learned with others who are struggling. This sounds strangely similar to a lot of what we have been talking about in this book, specifically *serving others*! Long before I decided to write this book, and way before my service opportunities with Instacart, the twelfth step of the *Celebrate Recovery* program was my favorite step. Most folks in our recovery group agree that the person who is offering to help another invariably receives the biggest blessing!

PERSPECTIVE:

So if you are counting, I have submitted a growing list of people that think it is a good idea to serve. That list includes the apostle Paul, many people in my twelve-step recovery group, myself, and I will add three others here: James, Joshua, and the Lord Jesus Christ.

JAMES

James, the half-brother of Jesus, opens his epistle by declaring himself a bondservant of God and of the Lord Jesus Christ; there is that word (bondservant) again!

> James, a bondservant of God and of the Lord Jesus Christ, To the twelve tribes which are scattered abroad: Greetings.
>
> *James 1:1*

I know what you are thinking: "If I were the half-brother of Jesus, I would serve Him as well." Not so fast! James never knew that his brother was the Son of God until after He was crucified—and that's kind of mind-blowing on many different levels.

If you are not familiar with the book of James, it is somewhat of a how-to book; many people refer to the book of James as a handbook for Christian living. The book is basically our marching orders on how to do life.

James not only declares himself to be a bondservant, but he is crystal clear on his instructions to us regarding helping others. In the passage below, James bluntly states that if you are claiming to be a Christian (James 2:14 is addressed to the brethren—that would be believers) if and you are not helping others—serving them—then your faith is dead. Ouch! Any questions?

What does it profit, my brethren, if someone says
he has faith but does not have works? Can faith save
him? If a brother or sister is naked and destitute of
daily food, and one of you says to them, "Depart in
peace, be warmed and filled," but you do not give
them the things which are needed for the body, what
does it profit? Thus also faith by itself, if it does not
have works, is dead.

James 2:14–17

JOSHUA

In the Old Testament, Joshua was pretty clear about his position in the matter of service, and he let the people of Israel know that it was, *first,* important to serve and, *second,*
it was critical to know whom they were to serve. The passage below lines out some clear instructions and warnings
about the subject of serving. In fact, there are no fewer than
thirteen references to serving in verses 14–24, highlighted
by the end of verse 15 stating these words: *As for me and my
house, we will serve the LORD.*

"Now therefore, fear the LORD, serve Him in sincer-
ity and in truth, and put away the gods which your
fathers served on the other side of the River and in
Egypt. Serve the LORD! And if it seems evil to you to
serve the LORD, choose for yourselves this day whom
you will serve, whether the gods which your fathers
served that were on the other side of the River, or the
gods of the Amorites, in whose land you dwell. But as
for me and my house, we will serve the LORD."
So the people answered and said: "Far be it from
us that we should forsake the LORD to serve other
gods; for the LORD our God is He who brought us
and our fathers up out of the land of Egypt, from

the house of bondage, who did those great signs in our sight, and preserved us in all the way that we went and among all the people through whom we passed. And the LORD drove out from before us all the people, including the Amorites who dwelt in the land. We also will serve the LORD, for He is our God."

But Joshua said to the people, "You cannot serve the LORD, for He is a holy God. He is a jealous God; He will not forgive your transgressions nor your sins. If you forsake the LORD and serve foreign gods, then He will turn and do you harm and consume you, after He has done you good."

And the people said to Joshua, "No, but we will serve the LORD!"

So Joshua said to the people, "You are witnesses against yourselves that you have chosen the LORD for yourselves, to serve Him."

And they said, "We are witnesses!"

"Now therefore," he said, "put away the foreign gods which are among you, and incline your heart to the LORD God of Israel."

And the people said to Joshua, "The LORD our God we will serve, and His voice we will obey!"

Joshua 24:14–24

JESUS

And finally, if you are still not convinced that serving is a great idea, please consider the following passage.

Just as the Son of Man did not come to be served, but to serve, and to give His life a ransom for many.

Matthew 20:28

So on its own, this verse should be a good enough reason for you to consider serving. Jesus came to serve, not to be served. Think about that: *Jesus came to serve!*

This could have been a way shorter book. Dare I say that we should serve for no other reason than Jesus did? But in context, the preceding verses say so much more about our human desires and tendencies.

> But Jesus called them to Himself and said, "You know that the rulers of the Gentiles lord it over them, and those who are great exercise authority over them. Yet it shall not be so among you; but whoever desires to become great among you, let him be your servant. And whoever desires to be first among you, let him be your slave.
>
> *Matthew 20: 25–27*

I strongly urge you to review verses 25–28 again and ask yourself these words: "Do I desire to be the greatest or do I desire to be the servant?"

The way I see it, the script will someday be flipped.

APPLICATION:

....

Choose to serve.

&

What Is My Purpose?

"I would prefer to just look at your resume."

For You formed my inward parts;
You covered me in my mother's womb.
I will praise You, for I am fearfully and wonderfully made;
Marvelous are Your works,
And that my soul knows very well.

Psalm 139:13–14

• • • • • • • • • • • •

So, this is it. This is how I will put a bow around every word that has preceded this last chapter and answer a question that individuals have asked for generations before me. What is my purpose?

I am not going to be the first to try to answer this age-old question. Volumes have been written long before my humble effort that you have graciously labored through to get the answer to this elusive question.

I could not possibly answer the question of what my purpose is until I address the question of who I am. To that end, who better to tell you who I am than the One who made me. Please take a look at who my Creator says I am.

PSALM 139

O LORD, You have searched me and known me.
You know my sitting down and my rising up;
You understand my thought afar off.
You comprehend my path and my lying down,
And are acquainted with all my ways.
For there is not a word on my tongue,
But behold, O LORD, You know it altogether.
You have hedged me behind and before,
And laid Your hand upon me.
Such knowledge is too wonderful for me;
It is high, I cannot attain it.

Where can I go from Your Spirit?
Or where can I flee from Your presence?
If I ascend into heaven, You are there;
If I make my bed in hell, behold, You are there.
If I take the wings of the morning,
And dwell in the uttermost parts of the sea,
Even there Your hand shall lead me,
And Your right hand shall hold me.
If I say, "Surely the darkness shall fall on me,"
Even the night shall be light about me;
Indeed, the darkness shall not hide from You,
But the night shines as the day;
The darkness and the light are both alike to You.
For You formed my inward parts;
You covered me in my mother's womb.
I will praise You, for I am fearfully and wonderfully made;
Marvelous are Your works,
And that my soul knows very well.
My frame was not hidden from You,
When I was made in secret,
And skillfully wrought in the lowest parts of the earth.
Your eyes saw my substance, being yet unformed.
And in Your book they all were written,
The days fashioned for me,
When as yet there were none of them.
How precious also are Your thoughts to me, O God!
How great is the sum of them!
If I should count them, they would be more in number
than the sand;
When I awake, I am still with You. [2]
Oh, that You would slay the wicked, O God!
Depart from me, therefore, you bloodthirsty men.
For they speak against You wickedly;
Your enemies take Your name in vain.

2 Italics added vv. 13 to 18 for emphasis.

Do I not hate them, O LORD, who hate You?
And do I not loathe those who rise up against You?
I hate them with perfect hatred;
I count them my enemies.
Search me, O God, and know my heart;
Try me, and know my anxieties;
And see if there is any wicked way in me,
And lead me in the way everlasting.

Very specifically, starting in verse 13 and running through verse 18, I am the guy that God formed in my mother's womb. I was fearfully and wonderfully made by the God who makes only marvelous things. Every detail of my body was skillfully attended to by God, and His eyes saw the creation that was me even before I was formed. God lined out the day that I was to be born and He knows the day that I will die. God's thoughts about me are precious. The God who created me knows what my purpose is.

For good measure, verses 1–6 tell me that God knows when I sit down and when I rise up, He knows my thoughts, and He knows the paths that I will travel. He knows my ways (*and He still loves me!*), and He knows every word that will come off of my tongue. He is protecting me from in front and behind, and His hand is on me. In short, He knows me better than I know myself.

In Genesis 1:26–27, my Bible tells me that I was made in the image of God.

Then God said, "Let Us make man in Our image, according to Our likeness; let them have dominion over the fish of the sea, over the birds of the air, and over the cattle, over all the earth and over every creeping thing that creeps on the earth." So God created man in His own image; in the image of God He created him; male and female He created them.

Genesis 1:26–27

Just for good measure Psalm 8 tells me that I am just a little lower than the angels.

> What is man that You are mindful of him,
> And the son of man that You visit him?
> For You have made him a little lower than the angels,
> And You have crowned him with glory and honor.
>
> *Psalm 8:4–5*

The fact is that I don't always *feel* like the creation that is lined out in the passages above, but I know that they are true, and it is at such times that I am reminded to rely more on my Bible and less on how I feel. The bottom line is that God knows who I am.

From time to time, it is probably a good idea to review not just who we are and what our purpose is, but to consider *where* we are. According to statistics, the average life expectancy for a male is 76.1 years. As of writing, I am 62 years old. There are a few ways to do this math: *First,* I might only have fourteen years left. *Second,* I can see behind me a lot further than I can see in front of me. Or *third,* I wish I had never searched out that statistic!

Maybe a sports analogy would be better. How about this: "If my life were a football game, I believe that I am playing in the fourth quarter." The truth is that I am fine if God sends a lightning storm and the game ends before the quarter, and I am also okay if the game goes into two overtime sessions. I do, however, recognize that the clock is ticking, and I want to make the most of every minute that I have left on this earth. I have been blessed beyond any man with a wonderful wife, a great son and daughter-in-law, and two grandchildren that are well on their way to changing this world in a big way, all in the name of Jesus Christ. I count it a tremendous blessing to know that when God calls me home, I am leaving this world with not a single regret.

One advantage of being sixty-two years old is that I can also say with a good measure of confidence that there are certainly a few things that will not happen before I finish my course on earth. With the complete understanding that God can do anything with my life, here is a short list of things that I do not believe I will attain before He calls me home.

I will not be:

- Ambassador to the United Kingdom or France;
- Heavyweight champion of the world;
- High-degree thief;
- Doctor or chief;
- State Trooper;
- Head of a big TV network.

Thanks again to Dylan for the list above; I love that song. Below are a few more things that I will never be:

- Best-selling author;
- Drummer for *Third Day*;
- As wealthy as Bill Gates; (Please note that I did not say as *rich* as Bill Gates. Because of Jesus, I am richer than Bill Gates.)
- President of the United States;
- Owner of a $1,000,000 RV that Rosemary and I will tour the country in for the rest of our lives. (Praise God, we still have our pop-up camper!)

Here is a short list of things that I would like to be as I live out my days:

- A better husband;
- A better father;
- A better father-in-law;
- A better grandfather;

- A better brother;
- A better Sunday school teacher;
- A better accountability partner and sponsor to my friends at *Celebrate Recovery*.

James puts my days on earth, my planning and scheming, into perfect perspective below. In summary, my life on earth is like a vapor; I am only here for a little while and then I will vanish away.

> Come now, you who say, "Today or tomorrow we will go to such and such a city, spend a year there, buy and sell, and make a profit"; whereas you do not know what will happen tomorrow. For what is your life? It is even a vapor that appears for a little time and then vanishes away.
>
> *James 4:13–14*

Without further delay, and I know you are dying to know,

"What is my purpose?"

At the risk of being anticlimactic (and I trust that you have already figured this out), I am here to *serve*.

I can't quite explain it, but after sixty-two years of scrambling and scraping, I have reached this conclusion that all I need to do for the rest of my days is serve. In reality, I did not reach any conclusions. God used a series of events over the course of some months to get my attention in a way that He never had my attention before. By allowing my "real" job to be replaced by a part-time shopping gig job, God revealed things to me that I most certainly never would have realized if I had continued on the same path without His intervening.

As an added bonus, and as it always is, God's timing was perfect. Six months before this all happened, I was consumed with the confusion and cares of this world—thoughts of when I would retire, what I would do when I retire, whether I would have enough money to retire. . . on and on and on this went. And then, in one moment, God allowed my "real" job to vaporize and most of those questions were answered. All of those questions were answered with one directive from God:

Serve.

PERSPECTIVE:

As we close our time together, it is my hope that you gained something from what I have submitted by way of this book. My desire has been to share a series of events that changed my thinking and, to some degree, changed the course of my life.

It took over six decades for me to realize the value of service—simple service to be more specific—and to yield to the concept of serving rather than merely being served. Having accepted this position of servant has changed me for the rest of my days.

My encouragement to you is for you to consider the same. Regardless of where you are in life, I am suggesting that the rest of your days will be exponentially better if you chose to serve first and let all of the other details of life come second. Please keep in mind that you should not do this because I think it's a good idea but because Jesus came to serve (Matthew 20:28).

If we claim to be followers of Jesus, we should do as He did.

APPLICATION:

Serve; it's simple!